Dear Janet!

I'm sending you the views of the nothern part of the Emerland Island → to the Emerald City in the Northern part of USA

— Magdalena —

Portrait of
BELFAST

RACHAEL CRAVEN

HALSGROVE

First published in Great Britain in 2009

British Library Cataloguing-in-Publication Data
A CIP record for this title is available from the British Library

ISBN 978 1 84114 842 7

HALSGROVE
Halsgrove House,
Ryelands Industrial Estate,
Bagley Road, Wellington, Somerset TA21 9PZ
Tel: 01823 653777   Fax: 01823 216796
email: sales@halsgrove.com

Part of the Halsgrove group of companies
Information on all Halsgrove titles is available at: www.halsgrove.com

Printed and bound by Grafiche Flaminia, Italy

INTRODUCTION

A Titanic Task

Belfast is certainly a city with a wide and varied history and the challenge for this book was to capture effectively the essence and atmosphere if its many different eras.

From early industrialisation, characterised by the boom in the linen industry, through to the world-renowned ship-building that took place at Harland & Wolff Shipyard, the city retains a visible record of its history. Indeed, in recent times there has been a growing drive to maintain the Victorian character of Belfast that is so evident to anyone visiting the city. The juxtaposition of this wonderful Victorian architecture with some of the modern glass and steel structures that have been developed in recent years makes for a very interesting canvas.

Of course, the regeneration of Belfast in the last ten to fifteen years is largely due to the end of 'The Troubles'. While it is clear to see that Belfast has moved on from this experience, there are also numerous opportunities throughout the city to capture images which glance back at the past.

Having lived in Belfast for ten years now I have watched it develop into a young, vibrant place and I hope that the images in this book succeed in portraying this to you. For far too long this place has not had an opportunity to showcase its interesting history and promising future. I hope this book provides Belfast with some of the exposure it deserves.

ACKNOWLEDGEMENTS

My sincerest thanks firstly to Andy Stansfield at Halsgrove for all his help and advice with this book. Giving me your mobile number was a brave decision!

Secondly, a big thank you to all the people who helped me get access to a variety of buildings and sites throughout Belfast – there are too many to mention them all but their help was invaluable.

A special thank you goes to Charles Lanyon. During my research for this book I discovered that this Victorian architect designed a large number of Belfast's most impressive buildings. Without his work the city would be a much poorer place.

Finally, thank you to my husband, Peter. A born and bred Belfast man, his knowledge of the city was a huge help and, without this, the task would have been considerably more challenging.

Flowers in bloom – spring flowers in the grounds of Belfast Castle, located on the slopes of Cave Hill, which overlooks the city.

A very Irish pasttime – Down Royal racecourse on the outskirts of Belfast has hosted horse-racing meetings since the early 1700s and is also referred to locally as 'The Maze' due to its proximity to the old Maze prison site.

City in a bowl – from the North Down hills on one side to the view of Cave Hill in the distance with the city sprawling in between.

Stormont Parliament Buildings – from the hills of North Down in the east of the city the
Parliament Buildings at Stormont dominate the landscape.

George Best Belfast City Airport – the city airport was given the name of one of East Belfast's most famous sons following his sad loss in November 2005 and is located less than 2 miles from the City Centre.

Left: Belfast Lough – looking north from the southern shore of Belfast Lough, a busy shipping channel leading to the famous Harland & Wolff Shipyard.

Church of the Most Holy Redeemer, Clonard.

Right: Clonard Church – located in West Belfast the Church of the Most Holy Redeemer was constructed in an early French Gothic style.

Spring has arrived – new daffodils on the Lagan Tow Path. A popular route for walkers and joggers along the River Lagan which leads out to the mouth of Belfast Lough.

Cooke Rugby Club – the home of the oldest Junior Rugby Club in Belfast
is now at Shaw's Bridge in the south of the city.

Down by the docks – scrap metal is loaded onto a barge on Belfast Lough
with the HSS in the background.

Left: Relaxing in Drumglass Park – one of Belfast's most popular retreats when the sun shines,
Drumglass means 'green ridge' or 'green hill'.

The Titanic Quarter – a view of the Bombardier factory at the docks with Belfast's two famous cranes on the left. These cranes dominate the Belfast landscape from wherever you are in the city.

RSPB Belfast Lough Nature Reserve – over 100 different types of birds can be seen here including Oystercatchers, Curlews, Godwits, Dunlins and Redshanks.

Thompson Dock and Pump House – where the RMS *Titanic* had its final fit-out. The pump house is one of the most significant remaining heritage buildings of the *Titanic* era.

Right: Belfast Lough – the southern shore of the lough.

The progress of human life – laser cut in sheet steel these
images chart the progress of human life from birth to
100 years old outside the Royal Victoria Hospital.

Right: Royal Victoria Hospital – completed in 1906 and laying claim to
be the first air conditioned building in the world.

The Palm House at Botanic Gardens – constructed in 1840 and designed by
Sir Charles Lanyon who also designed parts of Queen's University Belfast.

Left: HMS *Caroline* – the second oldest commissioned warship in the Royal Navy
is berthed afloat at the Alexandra Dock in Belfast's Titanic Quarter.

Ulster Museum – stone carving on the Ulster Museum building reflecting Belfast's maritime history.

Left: Inside the Palm House – originally constructed in the mid nineteenth century to allow horticulturalists to grow unusual tropical plants.

Signpost in Botanic Gardens.

Right: Queen's University Belfast – one of Belfast's most impressive buildings, Queen's University opened for business in 1849 and was designed and built by Sir Charles Lanyon. The University today has over 24000 students.

Donegall Place – Belfast's main shopping street in the centre of the city.

Flowers – one of Belfast's many on-street flower sellers on Castle Lane.

Royal Avenue – a view down Royal Avenue in Belfast City Centre with the Belfast Eye visible in the background.

Left: Coffee culture – alive and well on Belfast's Arthur Street.

Queen's University Students Union – the newly designed Union building
is in marked contrast to the main University Building opposite.

Belfast Print Workshop – dramatic mosaic and steel sculpture on this building, where professional print makers can access materials and equipment to help develop their art.

The Merchant Hotel – the former headquarters of the Ulster Bank, this Grade I Listed Building dating from 1860 has recently been developed into Belfast's only 5 star hotel.

The Cloth Ear – the public bar of The Merchant Hotel.

Kelly's Cellars – this bar in the centre of Belfast was a meeting point for the Society of United Irishmen, established in 1791.

Mourne Seafood Bar – one of Ireland's most renowned seafood restaurants, the menu varies daily depending on what is landed at the local fishing ports of Kilkeel and Annalong in County Down.

Right: Ulster Reform Club – originally established in 1885 the Ulster Reform Club shares this grand building with the Northern Ireland branch of the Institute of Directors.

A busy shopping city – a view down Donegall Place with Belfast City Hall visible.

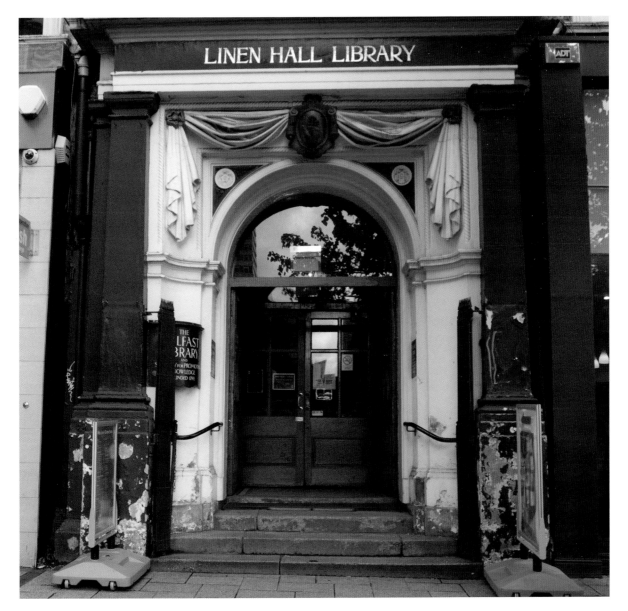

The Linen Hall Library – dating back to 1788 this is the oldest library in Belfast and the last subscribing library in Northern Ireland, relying entirely on membership fees and endowments for funding.

Belfast City Hall – completed in 1906, the idea was born following Belfast being granted city status by Queen Victoria in 1888.

Bank Buildings – now home to Primark, the Bank Buildings is a striking cast-iron structure clad in red Dumfries stone.

Boucher Retail Park – one of Northern Ireland's most popular retail parks
attracts visitors from all over Ireland – North and South.

Left: Bank of Ireland – this was the first art deco building in Northern Ireland when
it opened in 1929 but is today sadly unoccupied.

Botanic Avenue – a busy spot when the sun goes down due to a
large collection of bars, restaurants and live music venues.

Right: Victorian terraces on University Square – these buildings are owned
for the most part by Queen's University, located opposite.

The Empire Music Hall – one of Northern Ireland's most popular live
music venues hosting many bands and a well-known Comedy Club.

The Gasworks – the distinctive funnel and clock tower mark the site where Belfast's gas-making industry began production in the nineteenth century. Today, the site is home to a business park as well as the Radisson Hotel and enterprise workshops.

Stranmillis – a collection of art galleries, restaurants and the Ulster Museum can be found here.

C.S. Lewis – born in Belfast, this statue was erected in 1998 to celebrate the centenary of his birth.

St George's Market – one of Belfast's oldest and most popular attractions since the late ninettenth century, this building still hosts weekly markets for a variety of local produce.

St George's Market – view from outside.

Left: George Best 1946–2005. Pele Good, Maradona Better, George Best.

St Malachy's Church – when the foundation stone was laid in 1841
this was intended to be a new cathedral for Belfast.

Invest Northern Ireland – the headquarters of Northern Ireland's business development agency is one of the most impressive modern structures in the city.

The Odyssey Arena – Belfast's largest entertainment venue hosting live concerts, restaurants, a cinema and many bars. It is also home to the Belfast Giants ice hockey team.

Short Brothers offices – founded in 1908 Short Brothers were a former giant of the
world aviation market. The company was purchased by Bombardier in 1989.

Crawfordsburn Country Park – the popular coastal walk along
Belfast Lough in Crawfordsburn Country Park stretches all the way
to Bangor on the North Down Coast.

Left: Belfast Lough and Cave Hill – view across Belfast Lough
from Crawfordsburn Country Park.

McNeills Coaster – a step back in time at the Ulster Folk and Transport Museum just outside Belfast.

The Picture House – a recreation of an old Picture House
at the Ulster Folk and Transport Museum.

A rural scene – The Ulster Folk Museum was established in 1958 to ensure the people of Northern Ireland had a means of connecting to the way life used to be before Belfast became a major industrial centre.

Left: Ulster Folk and Transport Museum – set in 170 acres of rolling countryside on the outskirts of Belfast, the Ulster Folk and Transport Museum tells the story of life in early-twentieth-century Ulster.

Prize cattle – on display at the Balmoral Show
at the Kings Hall in South Belfast.

Left: Victoria Park – the park in the east of the city is home to a wide variety
of water birds such as swans, geese, ducks, herons and migrant waders.

Balmoral Show – Ireland's largest agricultural show is held every year
and attracts many visitors from all over the island of Ireland.

The King's Hall – located in the south of the city, many exhibitions are hosted here throughout the year.

The Mater Hospital – the original Victorian hospital building, which opened in 1883, is still in use today as part of a much extended hospital.

Right: Crumlin Road Courthouse – completed in 1850 the courthouse closed in 1998 and is an iconic image of the years of 'The Troubles'.

Belfast's murals – one of many murals that can be found all over Belfast depicting the political conflict that has been consigned to history over recent years.

Victorian-style lampposts.

Shankill Road Mural – the various political murals dotted around the city remain popular locally as a result of their artistic merit while also being a major attraction for visiting tourists.

Shankill Road – a view up the Shankill Road with the snow-capped mountains in the background.

An old linen mill – the linen industry was one of Ireland's most famous at
its peak and these old mill buildings can be found all over Belfast.

Two of Belfast's most famous buildings.

Belfast Royal Academy – the oldest school in the city having been founded in 1785, the school moved to this building in 1880 and remains at the site to this day.

Looking down to the lough – from the grounds of Belfast Castle on Cave Hill.

View from Cave Hill – looking down Belfast Lough
where it opens out into the Irish Sea.

Left: Belfast Castle – this dominating sandstone castle overlooks the city from
the slopes of Cave Hill some 400ft above Belfast Lough.

Malone House – an elegant late Georgian mansion set among the rolling
meadows and parkland of Barnett Demesne in South Belfast.

A view of the Belfast Hills from hockey pitches at the Sport Northern Ireland headquarters.

Two rowing boats at Queen's University Boathouse.

Right: Stranmillis House – set in 18 hectares of woodland close to Belfast City Centre this house is the main building for Stranmillis University College, a faculty of Queen's University.

Mary Peters Track – this track opened in 1975 and was named after Mary Peters following her pentathlon gold medal at the 1972 Summer Olympics in Munich.

Samson and Goliath – the names of the two shipbuilding gantry cranes that dominate the Belfast skyline. Goliath (1969) stands 96m tall while Samson (1974) stands 106m tall.

Union Theological College – founded in 1853 and today forms part of the Theology faculty at Queen's University. The college was also the home for the first Northern Ireland Parliaments while Stormont was being built.

Conway Mill – formerly a major force in Ireland's huge linen industry, Conway Mill is now a collection of craft units and local community development groups.

Dunville Park – one of Belfast's many parks, Dunville Park was donated to residents of the city by Dunville Irish Whiskey distiller Robert G. Dunville in 1891.

The Quad at Queen's – lies behind the main Lanyon Building.

Left: Clonard Monastery – Monastery of the Redemptorist order
on the Falls Road in West Belfast.

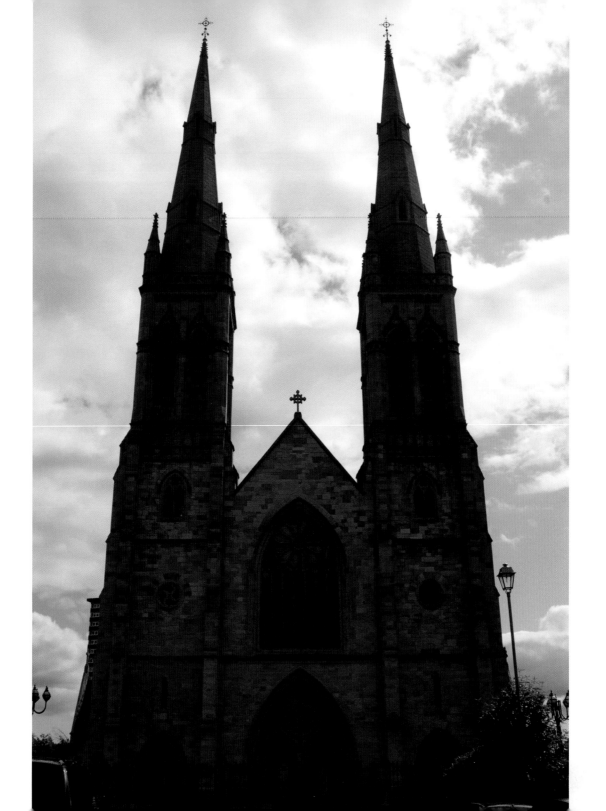

Belfast's parks – a large number of parks in the city offer a place to escape from the busy city streets.

Left: St Peter's Cathedral, Belfast – Gothic Revival style cathedral completed in 1866.

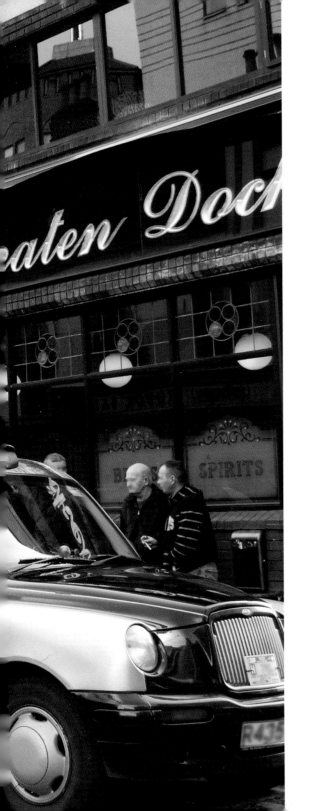

The Crown Liquor Saloon – one of Belfast's most popular bars, this Victorian Gin Palace is owned by the National Trust.

Left: Belfast's Taxis.

Robinson's – established in 1895, Robinson's houses a variety of different bars in this Victorian building.

The Grand Opera House – Northern Ireland's largest theatre, located on Great Victoria Street.

The Europa Hotel – one of Belfast's most famous hotels, located minutes from the City Centre on Great Victoria Street.

Right: Royal Belfast Academical Institution – a school founded in 1810 and still housed in the original building in the centre of the city.

Linenhall Street – Belfast's old Victorian tiled street signs were recently
re-commissioned by Belfast City Council.

Right: Belfast City Hall.

The Ulster Hall – re-opened in early 2009 after a major refurbishment.

Left: The Belfast Eye – offering spectacular views over Belfast and the North Down countryside.

Belfast Arts College – part of the University of Ulster which has four campuses throughout Northern Ireland.

Left: Broadcasting House – headquarters of BBC Northern Ireland on Ormeau Avenue.

Belfast Telegraph – published first in 1870 the 'Tele' remains Northern Ireland's most popular daily newspaper.

Central Library – this Victorian sandstone building was one of the first major public library
buildings in Ireland when it opened in 1888.

The Deers Head – one of few Victorian bars still open in Belfast City Centre having been in business since 1885.

Right: St Anne's Cathedral – houses the largest pipe organ in Northern Ireland.

Winter sun on Donegall Place.

Right: Pottinger's Entry – one of the city's five oldest streets, Pottinger's Entry was named after Sir Henry Pottinger, the first Colonial Governor of Hong Kong.

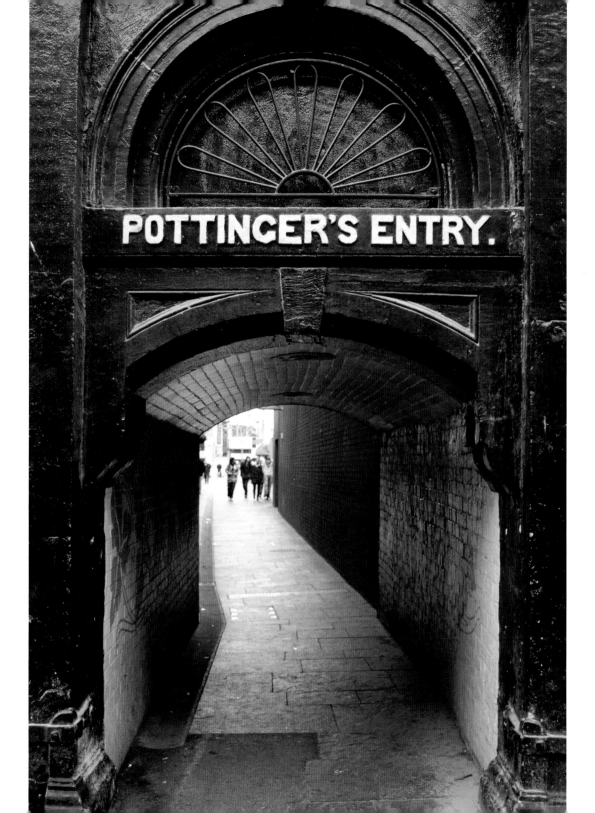

Street sculptures outside the recently opened Victoria Square shopping centre.

Victoria Square glass dome – this dome can be seen from all over Belfast.

Victoria Square and the Kitchen Bar – Belfast's newest retail development sits comfortably beside one of the city's oldest bars.

Right: The Jaffe Fountain – dates back to 1870.

IN REMEMBRANCE OF
DANIEL·JOSEPH·JAFFE
1874

Ornate Victorian lampposts on Bedford Street.

Right: Bittles Bar – a nineteenth-century triangular red brick building in the heart of Belfast.

114

Transport House – built in 1959 in striking contrast to the Victorian architecture that dominates Belfast.

The Albert Clock – this 43m high landmark was completed in 1870 and was built in tribute to Queen Victoria's husband, Prince Albert, who died in 1862.

Custom House Square – redevelopment of this space has transformed Custom House Square into a major outdoor entertainment and performance space.

Belfast's Fish – this sculpture was commissioned to mark the major redevelopment
of the Laganside area in the late 1990s.

The Lagan meets the Lough.

Ormeau Park – the oldest municipal park in the city, it was originally owned by the Donegall family, who gave their name to some of Belfast's most famous streets.

The Ring of Thanksgiving – symbolic of the regeneration and progress of the city as it moves onwards from its troubled past. Locally known as 'Nuala with the hula'.

Left: Queen's Bridge – opened by Queen Victoria in 1849.

Laganside – a major area of redevelopment over the last ten years.

Waterfront Hall – this major concert and conference venue on the
banks of the River Lagan hosts a wide variety of events.

The Barrel Man – commissioned by Bass Ireland in 1997
to mark 100 years of brewing in Belfast, this sculpture
can be found outside the Waterfront Hall.

Spires Shopping Mall – on Great Victoria Street.

Left: Wise words.

The River Lagan from the Annadale Embankment.

Left: St Peter's Cathedral interior.

Sir Thomas and Lady Dixon Park – home to the City of Belfast
International Rose Garden (when it's warmer!).

Easter Rising – a mural on the Whiterock Road in West Belfast showing the General Post Office on O'Connell Street, Dublin in the background.

Mural on the Whiterock Road.

Right: Dog sculpture in Falls Park – in reference to the tradition of greyhound racing in the area.

Ravenhill – home of the Ulster Rugby team.

Left: Falls Park – located in West Belfast and popular with children, families and local sports teams.

Giant's Ring Passage Grave – this tomb is believed to date from 3000BC.

Lagan Meadows – a place to escape less than 3 miles from the City Centre.

Wilmont House – designed by Thomas Jackson and completed in 1859, Wilmont House is located in Sir Thomas and Lady Dixon Park in South Belfast.

Ormeau Baths – the former Vicrorian swimming baths are now
an exhibition space for contemporary art.

A closer view of Parliament Buildings at Stormont.

Religious symbolism on Clonard Monastery.